Let's Go to the Barnyard!

2nd book in a Series of "Let's Go" Books

Presented by the Extended Weekends Magazines

Written by
Kandy Derden

Illustrated by
Dan Clevenger

© 2021 Let's Go To The Barnyard by Kandy Derden
ALL RIGHTS RESERVED

All names, characters and incidents, depicted in this book are totally the products of the author's imagination. Any resemblance to actual events, locales, organizations, or persons, living or dead, is entirely coincidental. No part of this book may be produced in any form, by photocopying or by any electronic or mechanical means, including information storage or retrieval systems, without permission in writing from both the copyright owner and the publisher of this book, except for the minimum words needed for review.

ISBN 978-0-9861109-9-3
Library of Congress Control Number: 2021943022
Published by Global Authors Publications / Filling the GAP in publishing
Printed in USA for Global Authors Publications

"Let's go to the barnyard," said Bradley.
"Okay," said Dexter. "Let's go!"
Bradley took Dexter to his farm near a town
called Beaman.

Bradley let Dexter out of the truck in front of the big blue barn and led him inside to a stall between a cow and a pig.

"Hello," said the pig. "My name is Bumper."

"Hi," said the cow. "My name is Belle." With her nose, she pushed some hay toward the sheep.

"Thanks," said Dexter taking a bite.

"I'd be glad to show you around," said Bumper.

"That would be great," said Dexter. "I think I'm going to like it here." He stepped closer.

"Oh, my!" said Belle and then she turned away. Bumper grunted, turned and bumped into the hay.

Dexter started to follow, but then stopped when he heard a noise.

"Who's there?" called Dexter.

"Boots."

"Where?"

"Here."

He spied a bronco eating from a bucket. "This seems like a nice place to live. I think I'm going to like it here." Boots didn't answer. "W-will you be my friend?" asked Dexter.

Boots lifted his nose out of the bucket. "Sure."

"Oh good!" said Dexter. "I finally have a buddy. My name is Dexter."

Boots sniffed the air near Dexter, snorted and turned away.

"What's wrong?" asked Dexter. Again, no answer.

Just then, some hay fell on Dexter's head. He looked up and saw a cat walking along the edge of the loft.

"Where did you come from?" asked the cat.

"Beaman," answered Dexter. "Bradley brought me in his truck." The cat started down the steps.

Dexter asked, "What's your name?"

"Buttons" she purred reaching the bottom step. "Who are you?"

"Dexter," he answered as he moved closer. Buttons stopped purring, stuck her nose up in the air, sniffed and ran back to the loft.

"Please don't go," called Dexter. But it was too late. She was already gone. So Dexter wandered out of the big blue barn.

"Hey," said a goat. "Who are you?"

"I'm Dexter," he said. "I hope I'll like it here." He paused. "What's your name?" Dexter stepped closer to the goat.

"Billy." The goat frowned, then lowered his head to butt Dexter with his horns.

Dexter ran away and hid around the corner of the barn behind a barrel.

"Whew!" That was close, he thought.

When a spider crawled past him, he was afraid to move.

"Don't worry," said the spider. "I don't bite. My name is Bitsy." When Dexter didn't answer, she continued, "You don't look very happy."

Dexter hung his head low. "I want to be happy here, but it's hard to make friends."

"Why?" asked Bitsy.

"I don't know," Dexter answered. "I haven't been here long enough to find out."

"I'll be your friend.
What is your name?"
asked Bitsy.

Dexter looked up
and moved closer.
Bitsy gasped. She
held her nose as
she scurried away.

Dexter spent the rest of the morning alone.
He watched a bunch of chickens playing.
A white chicken moved away from the others.

"Maybe no one likes her because her color is different," mumbled Dexter. "I wonder if that is why no one likes me."

"Are you new here?" asked the chicken. "How long have you been here? I'm Birdie. What's your name?"

Dexter wasn't sure which question to answer first.

Birdie continued, "There's a new rooster here at the big blue barn. His name is Boomer. He says he can crow louder than any other rooster. It's a good thing too."

Birdie continued, "Yesterday, Buck the mule tried to kick him. Buck doesn't like new people very well." Dexter decided not to go near Buck.

"When Buck's hooves came close to Boomer's head, he crowed louder than ever. It must have scared Buck because he hasn't gone near Boomer since.

"See that hen over there by the rain barrel? That's Biddy. Don't trust her with any secrets. She'll blab it all over the barnyard. Come on, I'll introduce you."

Birdie started to lead Dexter toward the other chickens. But after moving closer she sniffed, squawked and ran away.

Dexter found an empty corner of the barnyard beneath the shade of a birch tree and decided it would be a good place to think.

Hmm . . . being a different color didn't make any difference with Birdie. Belle, Bumper, Boots, Billy and Buck are big. Buttons, Bitsy, Birdie, Biddy and Boomer are small. So size doesn't seem to be the problem.

Being new isn't my trouble, because everyone was friendly at first. Maybe I'm not going to like it here, Dexter thought.

"Baa-aa," Dexter bleated. "Baa-aa. Baa-aa." He grew louder and louder.

"What's wrong?" asked a kind voice.

Dexter looked up at the biggest horse he had ever seen.

"No one here at the big blue barn likes me," he blubbered. "And I don't know why." Dexter didn't even try to make friends with the big horse.

Why should he bother?

"My name is Blaze," said the horse. "What's yours?"

"It doesn't matter," Dexter whined. "No one wants to be my friend once I tell them my name." He lifted his head. "That's it!" he said.

"They were all friendly until I told them my name. Baa-axter. My name is now Baxter!"

"Nice to meet you." Blaze picked up an apple from a bushel basket and dropped the apple in front of him.

Dexter came closer to eat the apple but Blaze backed away and snorted.

"What's wrong now?" Dexter asked. "I changed my name to start with a B just like everyone else." Dexter tried to follow Blaze, but he briskly walked away.

"I just don't get it," moaned Dexter as he began to wander around the big blue barn. He peeked around the corner.

No one was there.

He walked around boldly until he heard barking. A brown spotted dog breezed through the fence that bordered the barnyard.

"Hey, wanna play?"

Dexter blinked. "Are you talking to me?"

"Sure. Come on," said the dog. "I'm Buster. Let's go swimming in the pond."

"Are you sure you want me to?" asked Dexter.

"Aw, don't tell me you're scared? I do it all the time," Buster boasted.

The dog headed back under the fence. Dexter looked down at his dirty legs and feet. Maybe it would feel good to cool off in the water.

"Hey, wait for me!" called Dexter.

For the rest of the afternoon, Dexter and Buster swam and played in the water.

When they went back to the big blue barn, all the animals were under the birch tree.

"Hey, Dexter's back," said Bumper. "Come on into the shade."

"Where were you?" asked Buttons. Dexter was puzzled. Why was everyone so friendly now?

"My, you're all clean and white," said Belle when she saw him.

"And you smell good too," said Bitsy.

Suddenly, Dexter understood. "I was taking a baa-aath," answered Dexter.

"Nice," said Boots.

"Does this mean I can be a part of the family now?" Dexter asked.

"You always have been," said Billy.

"Dexter," said Blaze, "Now you look so good, you could win a prize at a contest."

"That's a great idea," said Bradley. "Let's go to the fair,."

"Okay, let's go!"

www.ingramcontent.com/pod-product-compliance
Lightning Source LLC
Chambersburg PA
CBHW081235020426
42331CB00012B/3184